The Story of Anna

By Lorraine Carlson Hammond

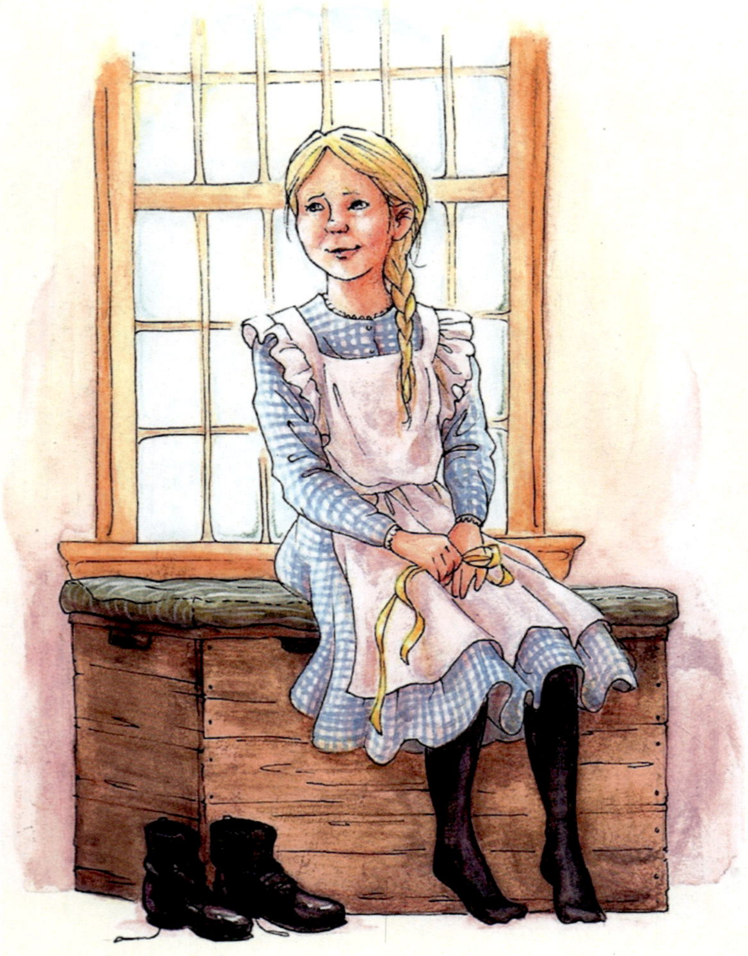

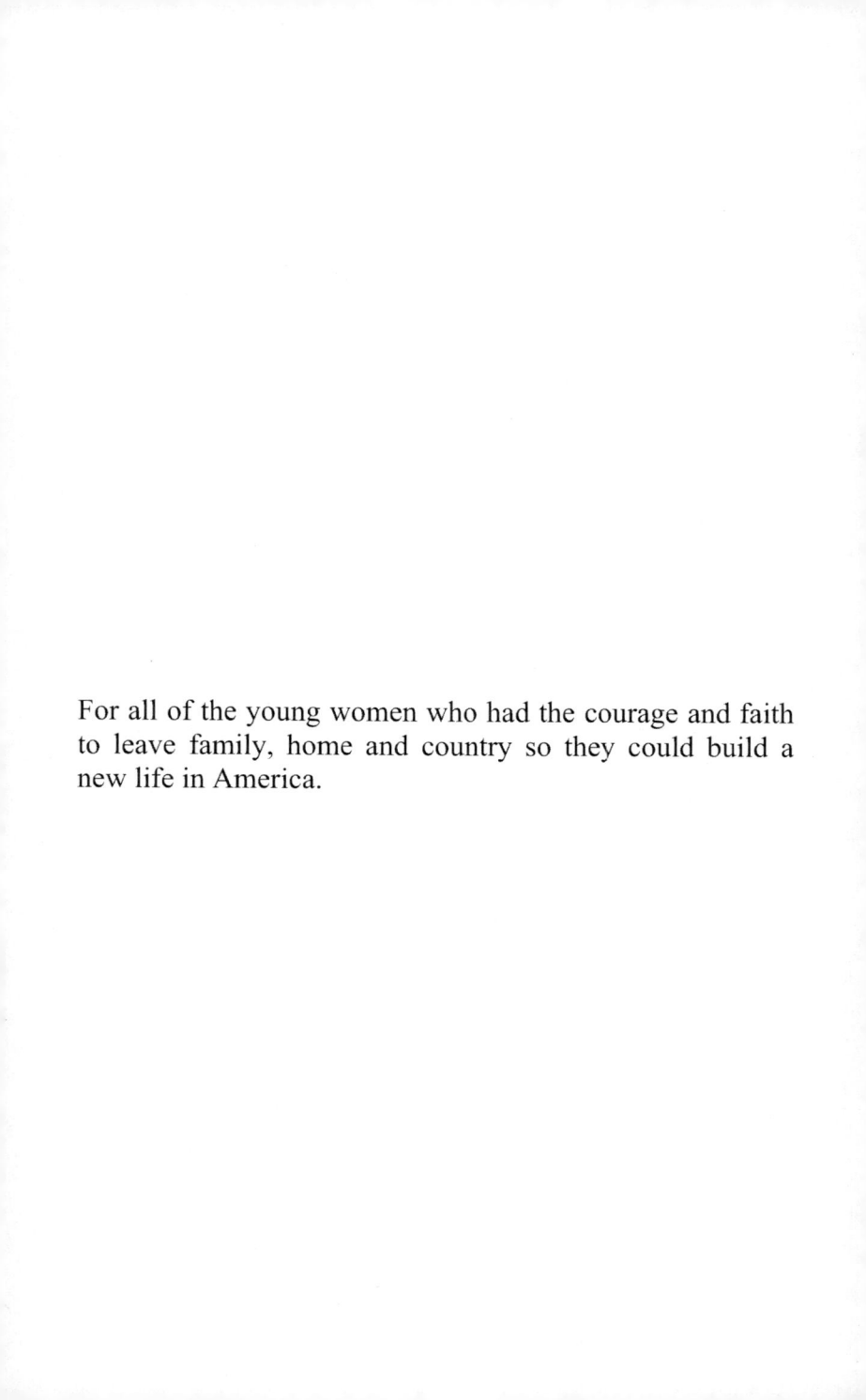

For all of the young women who had the courage and faith to leave family, home and country so they could build a new life in America.

Contents

1. Forward   2
2. Introduction   4
3. Farfar (Grandpa)   8
4. The First Day   14
5. Midsummer Celebration   22
6. Starting School   28
7. Gustop Torp - In Between Years   34
8. 'Good Jul' – Christmas Season   40
9. Anna's Conversion   46
10. Immigration   50

   Acknowledgements   56

Forward

This book is a novelette based on memories told to me as a young child by my Swedish grandfather. These memories have stayed with me all my life.

My grandmother, Anna Britta Lundstrom, was born March 6, 1866 in Vestra Vinagker, Sodermanland, Sweden. She was the daughter of Peter Erich Lundstrom and Britta Pehrson. She was one of nine children. Vingaker is a small village where the Swedish royal family had a summer home that the people of the village knew as "The Castle". Anna's father and the priest at the Lutheran Church, along with the school teacher, were the three most important men in the village of Vinagker. Peter Eric served as a farmer, contractor and builder, mayor, constable, and sometimes judge along with the priest. Anna's mother, Britta, worked in the castle as a cook. Their home was located on land that was owned by the royal family. It was larger than most village homes and was often a meeting place when Peter Eric had business to conduct. It was always called Gustop Torp by Farfar (Grandpa) and Mafar (Grandma).

Anna lived in the village of Vingaker for the first eighteen years of her life. Over the years, I have visited Vingaker, Sweden three times. I first saw Gustop Thorp with my father and his cousin Eric. The home was in same condition as when Anna lived there. During this first visit, I learned a great deal about the family and what it was to live and grow up in the village.

With these memories, and with later conversation with family members, as well as reading Anna and John's letters, it was easy for me to imagine the first 18 years of Anna's life. I have used the names of the family with researched dates, and descriptions from my visits. But it is not meant to be interpreted as a factual family history.

This book was written to remember and recognize the faith and courage of the many young converts to the Mormon faith that immigrate to the United States to help build "Zion" in the early years of the church.

Introduction

In 1935 our family returned to our home in Logan, Utah after living on the Ute Indian Reservation in Fort Duchesne, Utah for several years, where my father had been the county agent in Duchesne County. We returned because my father had decided he wanted to complete his education and enrolled in a doctoral graduate program. I had my fifth birthday in March, 1935.

That summer, on a day in mid-June, my mother woke me very early. I was surprised it was dark and still night to me. I remembered this was the day we were to take my father to Ogden so he could catch a train east to Madison, Wisconsin. He was to attend a PhD program in agriculture from the University of Wisconsin. I was excited, but also a little frightened. My family all sat down at the table and we ate our breakfast of oatmeal and fresh milk. Father offered a prayer asking for the protective spirit to be with him and his family this day and throughout the year while he was to be gone. Mother had fixed sandwiches and lemonade for us to have a picnic later that day. Soon Farfar arrived to go with us to Ogden.

When everything was finally ready, my family piled into our old Model A Ford car. Father drove, with mother in the front passenger seat. My older brother Leroy and sister Virginia and I were on Farfar's lap in the back seat. In the trunk of the car was the picnic basket and my father's trunk.

In those days it was not an easy drive from Logan to Ogden. We drove across beautiful Cache Valley and watched the sunrise over the mountains. The car started up the hill into Sardine Canyon. It was a steep and windy road and I was always afraid we would fall off the side. It took nearly two hours to reach Ogden. We stopped at a small park and had our picnic and then father drove to the train depot.

Father pulled up in front of the station and we all got out of the car. Farfar held my little hand tight so I wouldn't get lost. All of a sudden a large black man came up to my father, pulling a wagon, and put my father's trunk on the wagon. He was dressed in a maroon jacket trimmed with gold braid and big brass buttons, his cap was maroon with gold braid. I had never seen anyone that looked like him in my young life. He was taking my father's trunk away from him. I hid behind grandpa's leg and felt afraid. Farfar bent down and put his arms around me and explained he was a black man and that he was a called a porter. It was his job to put the trunk on the train so that it could go with my father. He assured me everything was alright and the porter was a good and nice man. The family followed the porter to the train. There seemed to be so many people rushing back and forth. There was not just one train but many trains on different tracks. Finally, we came to a huge new silver train that was very long. It was called the Challenger. This train was to take my father to Wisconsin.

Soon it was time to say our goodbyes. Father put his arms around each of us, told us to be good, to mind mother, and that he loved us. He then reached out to his own father. They embraced and said, "*Hej da och tack sa mycket* (goodbye and thanks very much)". Father then put his arms around mother and they said their goodbye. There were tears in her eyes and then, of course, my tears began to fall. Then a man in a dark blue uniform leaned out of the door of the train and called, "*ALL ABOARD!*"

Father climbed up to the steps onto the train, took his seat by the window, and waved to us. We all waved back and watched the train pull out of the station. I did not realize I would not see my father for nearly a year. Farfar looked down at my little face with tears rolling down my cheeks and said, "Don't cry *Lilla* (little one), I will take care of you while your papa is away." And he did.

Mother led the way back to the car and we all got in. This time mother drove, Grandpa was in front and I sat in the middle between my brother and sister on the back seat. Mother then carefully drove us back to our home in Logan.

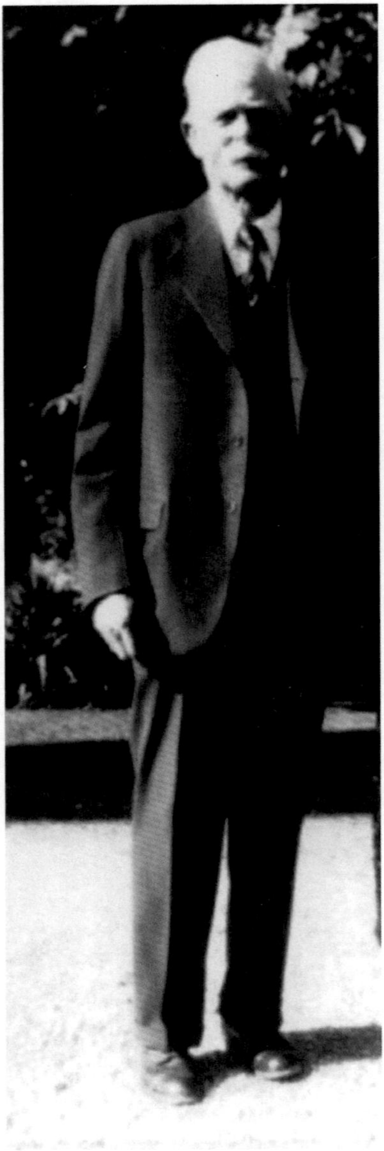

Farfar

Farfar was a tall man, and at the age of eighty he stood straight as an arrow. He had a head full of white hair and white bushy mustache to match. Most memorable were his sparkling blue eyes that would twinkle when he looked down at me. He always wore a black suit with a white shirt when he was not wearing his work clothes, which consisted of bib overalls, a flannel shirt, rubber boots, and an old straw hat. He was a kind, gentle, and dignified man.

Farfar had been schooled in blacksmithing and carpentry and had grown up on a prosperous farm in Sweden. He was very proud of his Swedish heritage. In his mind, first of all he was Swedish; second, a faithful member of the Church of Jesus Christ of Latter-day Saints (Mormon); and third, grateful to be an American. He appreciated the opportunities he had to work and to provide a good living for his family. A good education for his children was something that was very important to him and he always encouraged them to take advantage of opportunities that came to them.

The house my Farfar and Marfar lived in the last year of their lives was a big beautiful white Victorian house. Farfar had built a lovely garden surrounding the front and sides of the house. It stood next to the seventh ward meeting house in Logan. The rod iron fence between the house and the church had exquisite climbing roses. Gardens around the house were filled in the spring with crocus, daffodils, and tulips. In the summer, perennials such as peonies, bleeding hearts, iris, poppies, and annuals graced the garden bed. Sweet peas were the favorites because they would also climb the fence.

At the end of the garden were cherry and apple trees. Every space, including the large green lawn, was meticulously cared for. There was a hedge of yellow roses along the drive on the other side of the house that led to the out buildings. They consisted of a large white three-car garage.

Next to it was a root cellar where Farfar stored potatoes and root vegetables such as carrots and beets in a bed of sand. There were also squashes, pumpkins, and cabbages. This food provided for his family and ours through the winter.

At the end of the drive was an L-shaped barn. The first part facing the drive was his workshop where he could fix anything. It was here he kept all his tools. Then came the stalls for the cow he kept. Above the stalls and workshop was the hay to feed the cow. It was always a temptation to want to climb the ladder, made by boards nailed to the studs on wall. This was strictly forbidden by Farfar because he said it broke the grain off the stalks and left only straw which was not good enough feed for the cow.

In the summertime, the cow was kept in the pasture across the street on land Farfar had been able to homestead when he arrived from Sweden. It was edged by a canal fed by the Logan River, and there was a wire fence on the other side of the river and around the rest of the pasture. Farfar had planted apricot, plum, and apple trees along the edge of the river. There were lilac bushes and a black walnut nut tree planted on the side of the log bridge. There were enough wood planks on it for the cow to walk over. The nut tree and lilac bushes still stand today in place next to where a newer bridge crosses the water.

There was a long low shed, forming an L-shape attached to the barn where the chicken coops were. A high fenced yard was in front of the coops allowing for the chickens to forage during the day until they returned to their nests at night. As he did with the garden, Farfar kept this area very clean. Sometimes he would let me put a small linen bag of chicken feed over my shoulder and I go into the chicken yard and throw a little fist full at a time on the ground and the chickens would scramble around my feet and feed on it.

Over the summer, while my father was in Wisconsin, I spent most afternoons with Farfar. I was allowed to walk to his home by myself. It was a special and memorable time for both of us. Farfar always had white round peppermints in his suit pocket. Soon after I arrived he would take my hand and say "let's go outside". As soon as we reached the bottom of the steps by the back door he would give me a peppermint and we would walk around the shanty. This was the summer kitchen attached to the main house, around to the side of the root cellar. There he had built a bench where he sat to use his sharpening wheel. From the bench we looked out over the barn and his beautiful vegetable garden. The fruit orchard was to the side, so we sat in the shade. It was here on this bench that Farfar loved to share stories of his life in Sweden with me.

One day I said to him, "I know your name is John because it is the same name as my papa's, but what is Marfar's name?" He said, "Come *Lilli* and we will sit on the bench and I will tell you the story of Marfar. Her name is Anna. I first saw Anna from the deck of a ship looking down at the gathering of Saints boarding for the journey to England. Standing off to the side was a beautiful young girl looking somewhat anxious and alone. I fell in love with her the first time I saw her and I still love her." Thus began a wonderful summer, where sitting with Farfar on the bench looking out on his beautiful garden, I first heard the story of Anna.

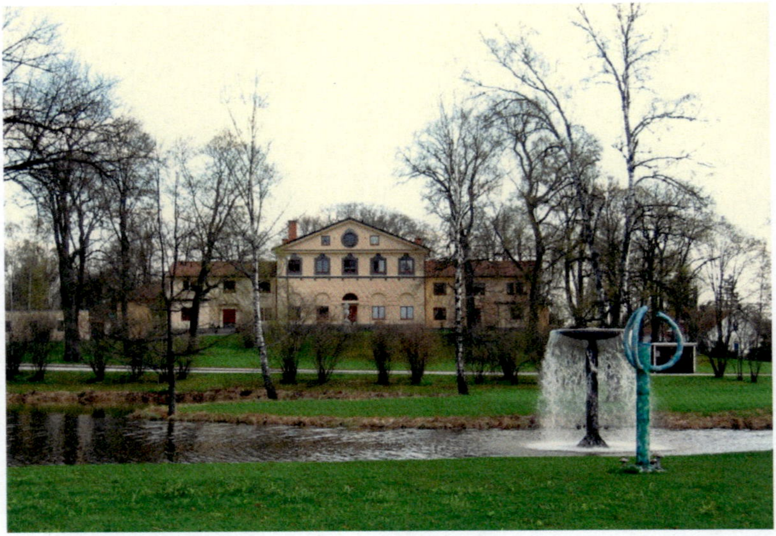

The First Day

Anna knew this was to be one of the most important day of her life. She had even been given a bath, her hair had been washed last evening before bedtime, and it wasn't even Saturday. She sat on a stool as her mother dried her hair and styled it into one long braid that lay at the back of her neck and down her back. Anna was a lovely child. She had thick blonde hair with just a hint of gold to it. She was small in stature with a beautiful round face. Her eyes were a bright blue. She had a small nose and rosy cheeks. Most endearing was her readiness to smile that easily twinkled into a laugh.

Anna's birthday 5th birthday was an important day, but that had already passed in March. Today was really important because this was to be Anna's first day to go to the Castle with her mother. Anna's bedroom was a small space over the kitchen that was warm both summer and winter. Summer was the time of the year when it really never gets dark at night. Anna slipped out of bed and was sitting on the window seat looking out across the red geraniums in the window box. Her older brothers were already working in the large field in front of their home. Papa was coming from the barn with the milk bucket having just finished the morning milking of the cow. Anna was already dressed for the day in all clean clothes. Her dress was not her best Sunday dress, but was a lovely gingham dress, navy blue with small white flowers. Over the dress she wore a white starched pinafore. The stockings were practical, long, and black. Shoes sat on the floor beside the window seat. Anna had chosen her favorite yellow ribbon for Mama to tie to the end of her braid.

Finally, Mama softly called up the stairs and said it was time for her to come down. They must leave soon. Anna quietly put her nightgown under her pillow, picked up her shoes, and slowly went down the stairs to the kitchen where Mama had her breakfast ready at her place at the table. There were two delicious buns and fresh milk. Mama tied a clean dish towel around Anna's neck so there would not be any crumbs or milk spilled onto the clean pinafore. Soon, Anna and her mother put shawls over their shoulders and boots on their feet. They put their shoes in a basket and started off to walk to the castle. It was a long walk across the field. They had to be careful to just walk between the rows of corn. The rest of the walk was a wide trail through a pine forest. The trail was damp with morning dew and covered with pine needles. They came out of the forest behind a big red barn with a large fenced pasture at the side of it. They walked between the barn and a low long building that Mama said was the tool shed, then into a big courtyard. Mama took Anna's little hand and led her to the big wooden door and down a few steps to the castle's kitchen. Anna felt both excitement and a little bit of fear now that she was finally going into the castle.

Although it was called a castle, it wasn't really a castle. It was more like a beautiful big manor house with a tower and a moat. Even so, the people of the village considered it a castle and called it that. It stood beside a stream with extensive well-kept gardens and two green houses. There were many out buildings including a stable, chicken coop, ice house, and wash house. The manor house was white with yellow trim and stood three stories tall. A curved drive crossed a bridge, then formed a half circle in front of the house, and back across the stream to the main road. The drive was edged with a low stone wall and in the middle of the half circle was a fountain that sprayed water up into the air. Anna had a hard time understanding how the fountain could do that.

They entered a long hallway with benches on each side with hooks above the benches. Mama hung their shawls on the hooks and they sat on the bench, put on their shoes, and tucked their boots under the benches. Mama then took from the basket a large clean apron and put it on. She had a smaller one she had made for Anna to wear on this first day as her helper. Then taking Anna's hand, Mama opened a door into a very large kitchen that had not one but two stoves and a fireplace large enough to roast a pig. There was a sink with a water pump right beside it. A long counter went down the middle of the room with copper kettles and other kitchen tools hanging from iron rods. At one end there were strings of garlic and dried herbs. At the end near the stove were hams and bacon hanging on hooks. Mama said this was to keep them from any mice or, for that matter, the cats that were supposed to keep the mice out of the kitchen. Now, the cats were sleeping on the hearth by the fireplace.

Another larger set of shelves contained more ceramic bowls of different sizes than Anna had ever seen. Mamma took Anna to the end of the big long counter where all the baked goods were prepared. It was across from two big ovens next to the fireplace. The ovens were like a stove in that there was a place to build a fire just under the bottom of the ovens. These had to be fed very carefully to maintain the right temperature for baking. The top of the counter was well-seasoned, smooth hardwood. Under the counter were bins of different kinds of flour, white, whole wheat and rye. There were big square tins of sugar -- white, powdered, and brown. At the back of the counter were two shelves with jars of spices: cardamom, cinnamon, cloves, and nutmeg, plus some spices Anna had never heard of. A big jar with a cheesecloth over the top contained the very important yeast that was needed for most of the baking. There were wooden spoons, whisks, egg beaters, different size cups, and rolling pins. At the side of the bins at the very end of the long counter was a cabinet with every baking tin and pan you could imagine. Mamma had every possible thing she needed to make all the wonderful baked goods she was so well known for.

Mamma brought a small stool and set it by the ovens and told Anna to sit there and just watch how things are done today. Then Mamma went to her counter and started to prepare the *vetebrod* (buns) for the day. No sooner had Anna had sat down when Mamma said, "Come with me now" and she took a big basket and bowl and they walked down the long kitchen back into the hallway. Instead of going outdoors, she opened a different door into a small room that was cool and dimly lit with only one small window. This is where the eggs, milk, cream, and butter were kept. Mamma took a dozen eggs and put them in the bowl, then put a round of butter and large jug of milk in the basket. "Now Anna, you are to remember where the things are in here because one of your jobs will be to fetch things I need from the cool room. You must remember to always to close the door tightly."

Back in the kitchen, Mamma put Anna's stool across from the counter where she was working near the ovens said, "Now watch what I do." She worked rapidly, mixing the eggs, butter, milk, cardamom, flour, and yeast into a large bowl. She covered it with a clean towel and set the bowl on a shelf near the ovens and started another bowl. As she worked, a young girl would gather any dirty dishes and utensils, take them to the big sink and wash them. She would bring them back for Mamma to use again. Soon the first batch of dough was ready to roll out and make the *Kringlor* buns that were shaped like a figure eight, as well as the round buns called *scorpa*. Mamma asked Anna to come over to the counter. She turned the dough out onto the floured wooden counter then took Anna's little hand and had her feel the dough. "*Sa har* (like this)" she said. Anna would remember the rest of her life how to feel if dough was "just right".

At lunch time, Anna sat at the small table at the end of the big kitchen with Mamma and several other kitchen workers. The children were given a slice of *scorper* bread, a hunk of cheese, and a glass of milk. The older people were served coffee from a big enamel coffee pot.

By the end of the day, Mamma had baked dozens of buns, some with cinnamon sugar on top and others with icing. She had also made a half dozen loaves of bread and two big bowls of custard. Now it was time for Mamma and Anna to go home. The big kitchen had been cleaned and made ready for the next day. They took their shawls off the hook and hung their aprons in their place. They put on their boots and placed their shoes under the bench. As they walked back through the woods and across the field, Anna could hardly wait to tell Papa about all the things she had seen and done.

Anna slept well that night, her dreams filled with visions of living in a castle. The next morning Mamma had to waken her and tell her to come and get ready again to leave for the Castle. This morning Mamma put Anna's small wooden clogs in the basket saying, "You will need those in the next few days."

During the next few weeks, Anna did indeed need her clogs. She became a real little helper to Mamma. She would bring in a bucket of small pieces of coal to keep the ovens going. She would get butter, cream, and milk from the cool room. Her favorite job was twisting and shaping the *Kringlors* and placing them on the buttered baking tins. Then, when they came out of the oven, she would sprinkle the tops with cinnamon sugar or paint them with white icing. She was always allowed to clean the empty bowl with a wooden spoon so she could lick away the last bit of icing.

Anna loved going to the Castle with her mother every morning that summer. She learned cooking skills that served her well the rest of her life. Anna also learned from the housekeepers how to manage a large household. Working in the Castle kitchen, she learned to speak High Swedish that she passed on to her children. High Swedish was the language of the royal family and those who had the privilege of having a higher education.

Anna's mother had worked in the Castle since she was a young girl and continued to work there during the summer months now only worked in the kitchen and was responsible for much of the baking that was done. Anna worked with her mother everyday through the summer and into the fall. It was that first summer that Anna had her first encounter with the royal family. The Royal Family came for several weeks each summer. They wanted their children to enjoy the countryside, the outdoors and nature.

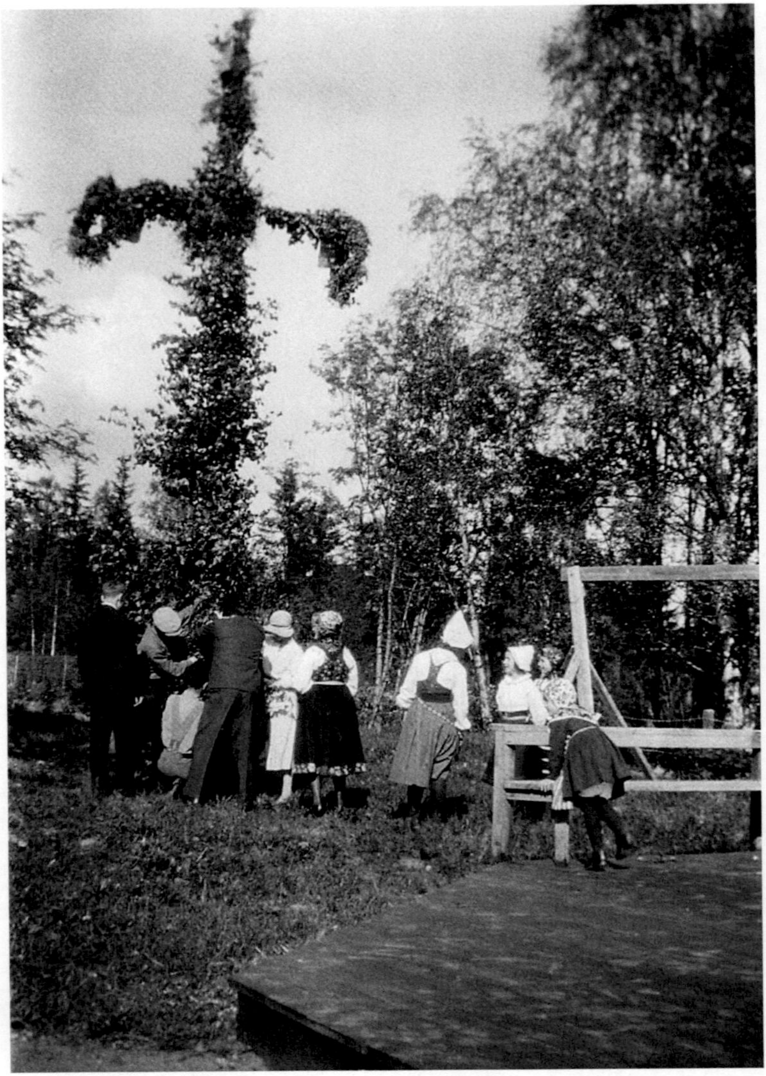

Midsummer Celebration

As the weeks passed Anna became familiar with the daily routine of the Castle. She felt she was learning something new each day. Anna made friends with the children of some of the other people from the village that also worked in the Castle during the summer months. There were not many children and most of them were older than Anna. She did make friends with one young boy named Karl, whose Papa was one of the workers in the gardens.

Sometimes Anna was sent out to the strawberry patch to pick berries when her mother needed them. Karl would help her and taught her how to pinch the berry by twisted it just right on the stem so it came off leaving the berry perfectly whole. Strawberries were an important crop each Swedish spring, especially for Midsummer's feast.

There was a lot of activity at the Castle when Anna and her mother arrived the second week of June. The windows were open and being washed inside and out. The curtains were being washed and would soon be hanging on the line fluttering in the breeze and sunshine. The carpets were brought out and hung on planks laid on saw horses and beaten with carpet beaters, that looked like huge fly swatters, to remove any dust. Inside the furniture was being dusted and polished, mirrors and chandeliers cleaned. The floors were scrubbed and waxed. The gardens were being weeded. The large grassy area near the stream at the side and back of the Castle was cut and trimmed. To Anna it seemed like the whole village was working at the Castle.

Mother explained that everyone was working to get ready for members of the royal family, Prince Oscar and Princess Sophie and their four boys, to come to the Castle for the Midsummer celebrations.

Midsummer is a celebration of the summer solstice which is the longest day of the year - usually on June 21st. It is a long tradition believed to go back to pagan times. It is considered one of the most important holidays in Sweden. Wild flowers were picked in abundance and wreaths were made to be worn by the women and girls and also hung on the Maypole. The Maypole is a large pole with a cross beam that is covered with greens and floral wreaths. The young men prepared a spot in the middle of large green area where there was room for dancing. They dug a deep hole and then raised the Maypole. There was a space at the edge of the green with stools and baskets of flowers prepared for the musicians. Large logs were rolled in along the edges of the green for the villagers to sit on.

The most important space was prepared for the royal family. A red carpet was brought out and unrolled in the place where they have the best view of the dancers and musicians. Chairs were brought out for the royal family. There were baskets of flowers decorating the area. Behind the logs closest to the castle were several large tables made by wood planks placed on sawhorses, then draped with white linens. Flowers were also used to decorate the tables.

The evening began with the food brought out and placed on the tables. There was pickled herring, new potatoes with sour cream, chives and new peas. Fish was grilled, usually fresh salmon from the nearby stream. The first strawberries of the year were served with fresh cream. The drinks of the evening were beer and schnapps for the adults and elderberry juice for the young. The food and evening were blessed by the village priest. The feast began with the royal family being served first, followed by the priest and the schoolmaster. The older people were served by the women from the castle and then the families came and fill plates for their family. Children were not allowed to take food from the tables.

After the feast musicians, which consisted of a few of the local gentry who could play a fiddle, harmonica, or a wind instrument or percussions of some sort, took their place. Prince Oscar gave the signal and the music began and the dancers took their places. The dancing again deferred to the old folks first some just holding hands, smiling and walking around the Maypole. Soon the families began to dance together around the pole. Anna's father swooped her up in his arms, swung her around once and then was joined by mother and her two older brothers. They joined with the other families and danced around the pole. There was always a round of applause when the royal children joined in the dancing. After a while the parents would break away and return to the logs and join the old folks who watched the dancers. At times they would sing along with the music, but mostly the women visited with one another, and the men stood around drinking beer or schnapps. The children danced until they were too tired to dance any more then joined their families and some would even fall asleep on mats and blanket spread out on the lawn.

When the festivities were over, the Prince and Princess and their young princes retired to the Castle, the chairs were taken in, the carpet rolled and put away until the following year's Midsummer celebration. Families slowly departed leaving the young people to dance until morning. Because it was summer Solstice it never really got dark that far north. A few of the mothers and fathers stayed on mainly to just make sure everyone behaved in a proper manner.

One of the traditions of the Midsummer festival was that young girls would pick seven varieties of flowers on their way home, put them under their pillow, and their future husband would appear in their dreams. This time of year was also a very popular for wedding and Christenings.

The following day was no longer a holiday, but a work day for the workers at the Castle. Everyone was a little tired but happy that the celebration had been such a success. There also a always a little sadness that there would not be another Midsummer for another year.

During the summer of 1872, there was a special excitement and tension throughout the whole village of Vingaker. Oscar II, Duke of Ostergotland, had become the King of Sweden and Norway. This would be the first visit of the royal first family. The big difference in this summer's visit was the king returned early to Stockholm and the queen and the children stayed on longer for the princes to experience the pleasures and joy of the summer in the country.

That year had another special day in Anna's young life. Prince Gustof, the new heir apparent, had his 14th birthday. He was eight years older than Anna she helped make his birthday cake. The traditional and favorite Swedish birthday cake was the *Jorgubbstarta*. Anna and Karl picked the fresh strawberries. She then cleaned and prepared them to decorate the top of the cake. Mother baked the cake and made the almond cream filling and the cake was ready to present to the young prince.

    Anna remembered this day well throughout her life and often spoke about what a privilege it had been to know and serve the father and son who became kings of Sweden. She had fond memories of them and of the times she played with the younger royal children.

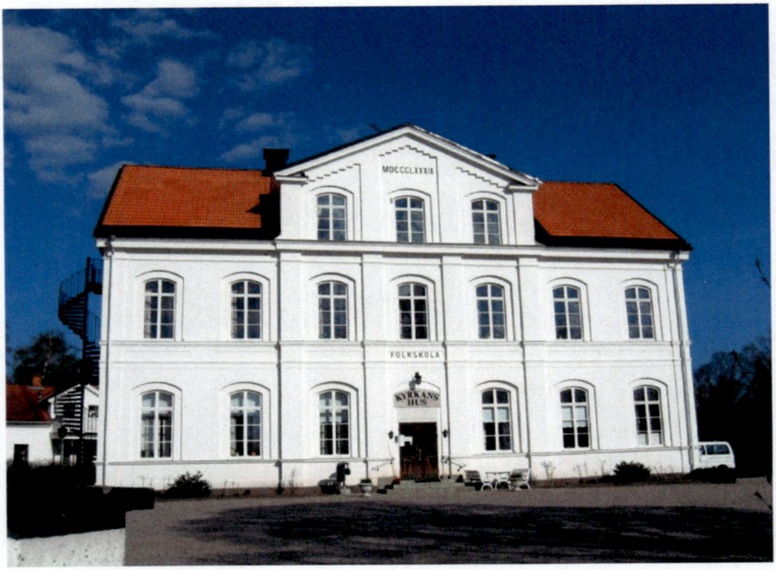
MDCCCLXXXIX
FOLKSKOLA
KYRKANS HUS

Starting School

Summer turned to winter and then the long, dark, cold winter finally melted into spring. The lakes and streams ran full, providing the needed water for the summer. The trees burst into bud and the snowdrops and crocus carpeted the ground. The windows of the cottages were opened, bedding hung on lines or over fences to air away the smell of the smoke from the winter fires that were needed for warmth and light in the cottages over the winter months. Wooden floors were scrubbed and polished, curtains washed and rehung.

In the barn, the cattle were turned out to graze on the new grass. Newborn calves and lambs began to appear. Gardens were planted. The longer days with more sun and warmth brought the spring.

Anna loved this time of the year. She thought spring was the time for new life and the best time of the year to be born. This year marked an important year for Anna for she had sixth birthday in March was now able to start school at the end of summer. Anna's two older brothers were already attending the village school. The school was several miles from her home but she wasn't concerned with this at the time.

Anna was fortunate to be living in Sweden where education for girls - at least four years - had became compulsory in 1848. In some schools where the schoolmaster was better trained and prepared, two or more years were offered. Boys in the larger cities had opportunities for vocational training. Boys from the upper classes of the society, including the clergy and politicians, were encouraged to attend the university.

Anna was eager to start school but it seemed a long time until fall and the beginning of school. Her mother reminded her the summer would pass quickly, as she was going to work with her again in the castle. In early May, Anna and her mother began their daily walk over the field, through the woods to the castle. Anna was given more responsibility this year. She worked mainly making the dozens of various buns that were made each day, the mixing of the ingredients, then feeling if the dough was just right. Then the dusting of sugar and cinnamon or the placing of the raisin in just the right bun. Her skill at baking was something she passed along to her children and grandchildren. She learned to anticipate when her mother needed and would get them for her without being told. She learned to read the labels on the shelves and containers where things were kept. This proved to be an advantage to her when she started school in the fall. Before long, the preparations for the royal family to return for their summer stay began as well as the Midsummer planning.

The summer passed quickly and Anna's thoughts turned to starting school. The school year began the third week of August. Anna was well prepared. Her brothers did their homework around the table with parent supervision. Anna watched, listened, and learned along with the boys.

Anna was used to getting up early and leaving the home but this would be the first time it would not be with mother. She would be on her own. Of course, she went with her brothers but when they arrived at the school she was separated and sent to the front of the classroom with the new students. Anna again had the advantage in that she knew the teacher. He was a friend of her father and had been in their home. Anna was a good student, eager to learn. She already knew some of the students from church and soon made new friends.

The schoolhouse was a large building adjacent to the church. It was also used for community meetings and social events. The schoolmaster occasionally had help from the priest, older students, and parents. Vingaker was a small village and the number of students was not large, making it possible for each student to receive individual attention. Anna also had the advantage in that both of her parents had been educated and encouraged and supported their children in their studies.

Anna and her brothers were used to the long distance to the village square where the church and school house stood. Many mornings Pappa hitched up the wagon and drove the children to the school house. The younger students weren't required to spend as many hours in the classroom as the older students. Anna began the long walk home with friends but finished the walk alone. When winter came, her older brothers skied to school and, until Anna could ski, they pulled her on a sleigh. During the winter months, Anna waited until the school day was over so she could return home safely with her brothers. When she completed the required 4 years for young girls to be in school, she was allowed to continue her education.

By 1879, Peter Erik had finished school and started working the farm with Papa. Carl turned fifteen, finished school, and was sent to Stockholm to learn to be a carpenter. Anna was thirteen and was needed at home and so her school years came to an end.

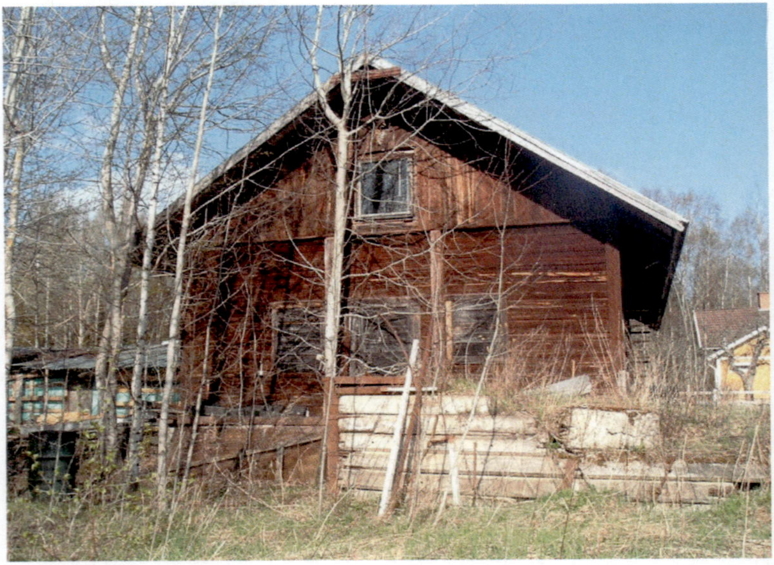

Gustop Torp - In Between Years

The Lundstrom home where Anna was born and raised in was a lovely, typical Swedish home of the 1800s. It consisted of two rooms on the first floor and the upper level under the roof divided into two sleeping areas.

The ground floor was the heart of the home. A stone hearth divided the area making a small sleeping area for her parents. This area was sometimes called the birthing room.

They were fortunate to have a stove adjacent to fireplace. They had no electricity or running water. There was a pump for water just outside the door that provided water year-round from a deep well. A little path to the side of the house tucked away in the birch trees led to the *privie* or the outdoor toilet.

Anna's father built all the furniture and her mother braided beautiful rag rugs from fabric scraps that could not be used for anything else. Some of the scraps for the rugs came from cast off drapes and clothing by the castle. During one of Father's trips to Katrineholm, he bought a small mirror that was considered a luxury. Anna grew up on a loving, happy home. It was a religious home where they taught high moral standards and the importance of education.

The years between 1862 and 1879 brought many changes and to Anna's family. These years brought good times as well as times of sadness. The family consisted of two older brothers, Peter Erick, born in August 1862, and Carl Fredrik, born in September 1863. Anna had two younger brothers Andrew Gustof, born April 1868, and August Leander, born October 1870.

During the summer months when Anna and her mother worked at the castle, hired help came each day to care for the younger boys and work in the home. The older boys began to work alongside Father at an early age. As was the custom, the main meal of the day was midday. During the summer months, Anna and her mother ate at the castle. Father and the boys came in from the field and their meal was prepared by the hired help. The family larder was supplied from fruits and vegetables grown on their farm, eggs from their chickens, milk from their cow, and occasionally wild game. Flour came from the wheat grown on the farm and ground in the community mill. Sugar, coffee, salt and spices were commodities that had to be purchased.

The days were long in the summer allowing the men to work long hours in the fields. As Anna and her mother returned home in the evening and cross the field, Father called the boys and they would all returned home together. While Father and the boys washed and cleaned up in the trough by the water pump, Mother and Anna prepared the evening meal. It usually consisted of bread and milk and in the summer, lingonberries that were picked in the woods at the side of their cottage. The family always ate together. Gathered around the table, Father would offer a prayer of thanks. It was a time for the parents and children to share the events of the day. After the meal the children played games in the yard, swung from the tree swing, and if the boys were fortunate enough to have a ball they played with it. During the school year began, time after the evening meal was spent doing school work. Sometimes Father would read to the family from the bible.

In November 1872, a second girl, Matilda, was born. It was a time of great joy for the family. Anna was especially pleased to have a baby sister. Matilda was a small baby and it soon became apparent that she needed extra care. Anna did all she could to help her mother and the new baby over the next few weeks and months. Anna helped prepare the evening meal and cleaned up afterwards. When Matilda was old enough to leave the cradle, next to her parents' bed, she shared Anna's bed. They became very close. Matilda was a pleasant child, never complaining even though she was very often ill. There were no doctors to consult with, only the local midwife.

In May 1878, Anna's mother gave birth to twins, Elin and Selma. Anna's mother's health began to fail after the birth of the twins and from all the extra care Matilda needed. The stress of caring for sick children had taken a toll on the family. When Anna was thirteen, the twins died on April 9, 1879. Six weeks later Anna's beloved little sister Matilda also died on May 30, 1879.

Anna struggled with her faith and felt angry and confused with God. Why had he not answered her prayers and taken her beloved little sister and the twins? Her parents helped her to accept and to come to peace with their deaths. They had been through this before when they lost their third baby boy, August, in March 1865. He lived only a month. Matilda and the twins were buried in the graveyard surrounding the beautiful Lutheran church in the village. Anna and her family often visited the graves after Sunday services in the summer and placed flowers on the small graves.

By 1879, Anna was thirteen years old. Much of the heavy work of managing the home became Anna's responsibility with Mother's supervision.

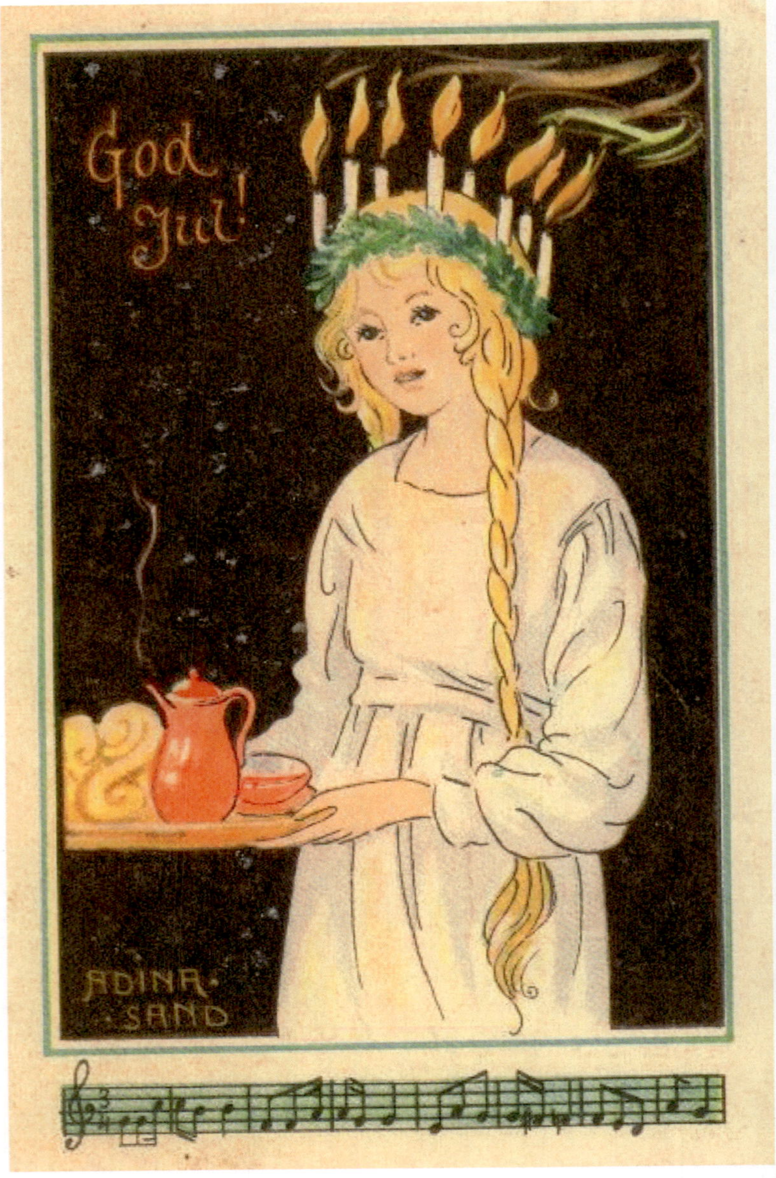
God Jul!
ADINA·
·SAND

'God Jul' - Christmas Season

Christmas is the most important holiday of the year in Sweden. The days are short and the nights are long and dark. Where Anna lived, on a good day there are roughly six hours of daylight. The village school would close from mid-December until St. Knut's Day, January 13th, the 29th day of Christmas.

December 13th is near the time of the winter solstice -- the shortest day of the year. Sweden had turned an old pagan festival of lights into St. Lucia's Day which marked the beginning of the month-long celebration of Christmas. St. Lucia's Day begins with the youngest daughter in the family, usually about 12 years old, dressing in a long white gown with a red sash. She will wear a crown of lingonberry branches with tall lit candles. The boys of the family can dress as star boys with long white shirts and pointed hats. They awaken their parents and serve them coffee and *lussekatter* (Lucia Day buns).

For Anna, the village and school closed on St. Lucia Day and a procession was held. The other girls who were not Santa Lucia dressed in long white gowns and red sashes, but no crown. The boys accompanied them, dressed as star boys. They sang carols and finish the procession at the church where they were treated to lucia buns or gingersnaps.

In Anna's village, St. Lucia's Day was mostly celebrated in the home. If a family did not have a daughter or one old enough to be St. Lucia they would combine with friends and neighbors. When Anna was ten-years-old, as Christmas approached her mother told her that this year she was old enough to be St. Lucia in their own home. Preparation for this day required the family working together for days ahead. Mother helped with the white gown and red sash. Her older brothers, Peter Erik and Carl Fredrick, gathered the evergreens and made the crown with father's help, to provide and secure the candles. Anna helped the boys make their pointed hats and star wands. The boys would wear new white nightshirts Mother made. The day before, Anna and her mother made the St. Lucia buns.

Anna excitedly counted the days until the 13th of December. Finally, the day arrived. Anna arose early, went down to the kitchen area, made fresh coffee, arranged a plate of Lucia buns on a plate, cups and saucers and placed them on a tray. She then went back upstairs and dressed in her beautiful new white gown. Her brother Erick tied the sash, secured the crown, they were all ready and went quietly down the stairs. Erick carefully lit the candles. Anna added the coffee to the tray, and they went the few short steps to their parent's small bedroom. Mother and Father had been waiting with anticipation but acted surprised when Carl knocked and opened the door and announced Saint Lucia. The whole family, including two-year-old Gustof and new baby August, gathered on the bed and enjoyed Lucia Buns. Christmas had begun.

A small Christmas tree was usually put up a day or two before Christmas. The decorations were a few candles in a little metal holder that would clip onto the branches of the trees. These little holders were saved from year to year and even handed down in a family. Swedish flags, strings of berries, and handmade straw ornaments were carefully hung by the children with Mother's help. When the time came to light the candles, it was always Mother's job.

Christmas Eve is also very important in Sweden. The *julafton* meal or smorgasbord is the main Christmas feast. Christmas Eve was a very festive day shared with extended family, friends and neighbors. The house was decorated with candles and the Christmas tree. There was the smell of freshly baked ginger cookies. The smorgasbord takes many days to prepare. It usually included *julskika* (a Christmas ham), meatballs, jellied pig's feet, *lutfisk* (a dried cod served in a white sauce), vegetables including red cabbage, beets, and potatoes baked in cream, onions and anchovies. A special bread was made ahead that is dipped in the juice from the ham. To finish the meal there was a selection of homemade sweets and pastries. The favorite and traditional dessert was *risgrynsgrot* a baked rice pudding that was eaten with raspberry jam and a sprinkle of cinnamon. Most of the time this was served after the presents are opened. The feast lasted most of the afternoon. To wash all the food down there was coffee and *glogg*, a sweet mulled wine.

Christmas Eve was the traditional time that presents are exchanged. The presents were placed in a bag and placed under the Christmas tree. They were distributed by a member of the family dressed as *tomte* or a Christmas gnome. Gifts were simple and homemade, new warm mittens, socks or hat. Each child received a little bag with a few nuts and dried fruit and sometimes an orange. The younger boys received a wooden toy carved by Father. The girls, a small rag doll with clothes made by Mother.

Christmas Day began with the family attending church. It was a day to enjoy the good food from the day before, the gifts received, and a day of rest. The Christmas season traditionally ended on the 20th day after Christmas. The decorations that could be used next year were packed away and the candy and apples the trees. The neighbors brought their trees to an open space in a field and set fire. Another '*God Jul*' for Anna and her family had been celebrated.

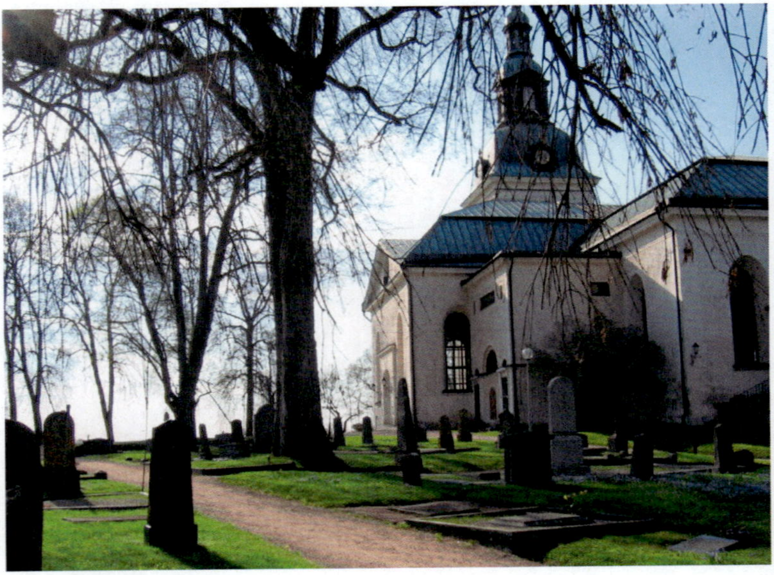

Anna's Conversion

The Lundstrum family had recognized religious beliefs as an important part of their life. They were faithful and devout members of the Lutheran church. Each Sunday, in good weather, they walked the five miles into the village to attend services and bible studies. The Lutheran church in Vingaker was, and still is to this day, a very beautiful church that stands on a knoll just to the right of the school house in the heart of the village. The church is surrounded with stately old trees, gravestones and paths lined with small shrubs and flowers. Many of Anna's ancestors are buried there.

The priest was a stern, well-educated man, yet kind and concerned with the welfare of the members of the parish. In a village as small as Vingaker the single religion was Lutheran, occasionally missionary from other sects would come in the village.

The first Mormon missionaries arrived in Sweden in June 1850. Within a few years more missionaries were called to Sweden. The membership spread slowly. The women who joined the church became the strength of the church. The first person to join the church from Vingaker was Britta Olsdotter Persson. She encountered missionaries in a trip to Stockholm in 1877. Through her work to promote the church a small branch was established in Vingaker.

When Anna was about 16 years old, she and her mother were walking home from church services and they passed a small cottage. They heard beautiful singing, they went closer and saw that it was two young Mormon missionaries that were singing the hymn "Oh My Father". They decided all the vicious stories and rumors of the Mormon missionaries could not be true.

The missionaries traveled without "purse or script". They were dependent on members to provide for them. When two young missionaries came to their home Anna's mother gave them a meal and allowed them to sleep in the loft of the barn. In the evening, members of the family listened to their teaching.

Mother was no longer working at the castle as often. Sweden was affected by the great depression that swept across America and Europe. There was unrest between the peasants and government over taxes and ownership of the land. Uncertainty of the times weighed heavily on Anna's mother's mind and she worried about what future there was for her family. She found comfort in the teaching of the young Mormon missionaries and was the first in the family to be converted. Soon after, Anna at age seventeen was converted and was baptized in the river near the castle.

The Mormon church like other churches in Sweden was encouraging new converts to the church to immigrate to America by offering free passage to America. For Mormon converts they were immigrating to Zion.

When the local priest learned of Anna's interest in Mormon church, he came to see her in the family home. He was very disturbed and concerned that both mother and daughter were investigating the church teachings. The Lundstroms were such stalwart members in the congregation. Many of the young people of the village, especially the young men saw a chance of new life with more opportunities and opted to take advantage of it. The priest understood the exodus of the young people and had great concern about the changes in his congregation.

Vingaker was no longer the thriving village of the eighteen sixties, the population was decreasing, the king and his family no longer came in the summertime. Other members of the royal family still visited the castle occasionally.

S.S. WISCONSIN, 1870 Guion Line
Courtesy The Peabody Museum of Salem

Immigration

As Anna turned seventeen in March 1873, her family began to think that Anna should be the first to immigrate to the America and help build "Zion". The Mormon Church, as well as other churches in Sweden, were offering free passage to America. Young Swedish girls were very desirable with Swedish families. They were educated, were good nannies, and had cooking skills. They very often were able to arrange in advance a position with a family in the state of Utah.

Father and Mother recognized there was little opportunity for Anna in Vingaker. Many of the young men had left, either to the large cities or America. The population of young people in Vingaker was decreasing rapidly. The life of Anna's childhood was coming to an end.

It was a difficult decision for the family to tell the missionaries to try and find family in American that would take Anna as help. Once the decision was made, Mother and Anna prepared what she would need to take with her on her journey to this new land. Father built a small wooden trunk for her. It took months for the correspondence to reach the church headquarters in Salt Lake City, Utah, to find a suitable family, and then get word back to Sweden. Finally, in the summer of 1884, a letter came from a family in Grantsville, a small town west of Salt Lake City, near the Great Salt Lake saying they would take Anna. This was a barren area on the edge of the great western desert so very different from Sweden.

Anna was excited when the news came, but she also felt a deep sadness to leave her family, friends and beautiful farm home. She felt frightened to leave the security of family, home, and country she loved. In eighteen years, Anna had never traveled outside of Vingaker.

The documents and instructions for Anna's passage arrived in August. Father and her brother loaded the wagon with her trunk. Mother had prepared a basket with food for the journey. They drove into the village to the train station to wait for the train to Gothenburg. Anna didn't know that she would never see her mother or her older brothers again, or ever return to Sweden.

Gothenburg was not a long journey, only about forty miles from Vingaker. There Anna joined with a company of Mormons waiting to board a ship to Liverpool, England. It was not a large ship but it had a short gangplank lead up to the deck where the company began to board the ship. This is where Farfar first saw and fell in love with Anna.

John (Farfar) was born on June 28, 1859 to Carl Gustaf and Anna Marie Jonasson in Lanpaskede, Jonkoping, Sweden. John's brother and sister both died as children. When John was 16 he finished his education and was sent to Stockholm to learn a trade - this was the custom at that time in Sweden. It was in Stockholm that John learned the trade of a Blacksmith.

As John was preparing to go to Stockholm his father became very ill. John sat by his father's bedside while his father told his son his thoughts and concerns, "Son, all my life I have been searching for something, I know not what, something that will make our lives richer and more meaningful and will give a deeper meaning to our religious faith. Son, seek always for such truth, and when you find it, remember Mother and me and your brother and sister." After his father died John went to Stockholm. Not long after he arrived in Stockholm his mother died. John had lost his entire family.

John met Mormon missionaries in Stockholm and converted to the faith and felt "surely, this must be the truth about which his father spoke of". When he had saved enough funds he decided to leave his beloved country and immigrate to "Zion" with the latter-day saints. He left Stockholm and went to Gothenburg to joined a group of other Mormons emigrating to Salt Lake City, Utah.

John August Carlson stood at the railing of the deck and looked down and saw a beautiful young girl, standing off to the side, looking reluctant and frightened. He felt an immediate attraction for her and went to assist her board the ship. Anna shared the provisions in her basket with John. This was the beginning of their courtship.

Liverpool was the most popular immigration port in Europe. It was teaming with immigrants from all over Europe. Anna was grateful for John's help and protection as they waited for the steamer that was to take the small company of Mormons to America.

In August, they set sail on the ship *Wisconsin*. It took six long weeks to cross the Atlantic. John and Anna became well acquainted in those six weeks and then on the long train ride to Utah. When they arrived in Salt Lake City, Anna went to Grantsville with a family her parents had known in Sweden. John went to Logan, Utah.

John and Anna corresponded and it was not long until John persuaded Anna to come to Logan. There Anna worked as a cook for a well-to-do English family that lived on the hill near the Logan Temple. The mother of the family would tell Anna what she would like for dinner in English and the young daughter would show her what was wanted. This is how Anna began to learn English.

John and Anna were married November 10, 1886. They were married by Apostle Marriner W. Merrill in the beautiful Logan Temple.

Two young people who had the courage and faith to immigrate to America, met and fell in love during their journey. They married, became parents to ten children and built a wonderful live together in a country far away from where they were born and raised. I'm grateful to be a descendant of such courageous immigrants.

Acknowledgements

My thanks for everyone who encouraged and helped me in putting the book together. Everyone who helped are direct descendants of Anna and John, either by birth or through marriage. I would like to extend a special thanks to Barbara Gross Hammond, Catherine Hammond, Diane Tueller Pritchett, Emily Hurst Pritchett, Kate Hoffmire, Nancy Cook, Peter Carroll, and Shelley Hoffmire. An extra special thanks to Emily for the illustration of Anna.

Made in the USA
Middletown, DE
06 March 2019